ANYTHING AND
ITS SHADOW

Anything and Its Shadow

POEMS

Lucie McKee

GREEN WRITERS PRESS *Brattleboro, Vermont*

Printed in the United States

10 9 8 7 6 5 4 3 2 1

Green Writers Press is a Vermont-based publisher whose mission is to spread a message of hope and renewal through the words and images we publish. Throughout we will adhere to our commitment to preserving and protecting the natural resources of the earth. To that end, a percentage of our proceeds will be donated to environmental activist groups. Green Writers Press gratefully acknowledges support from individual donors, friends, and readers to help support the environment and our publishing initiative.

green writers press

Giving Voice to Writers & Artists Who Will Make the World a Better Place
Green Writers Press | Brattleboro, Vermont
www.greenwriterspress.com

ISBN: 979-8-9904801-9-3

PRINTED ON 100% PCW RECYCLED PAPER BY BOOKMOBILE.
BASED IN MINNEAPOLIS, MINNESOTA, BOOKMOBILE BEGAN AS A DESIGN AND TYPESETTING PRODUCTION HOUSE IN 1982, AND STARTED OFFERING PRINT SERVICES IN 1996.
BOOKMOBILE IS RUN ON 100% WIND- AND SOLAR-POWERED CLEAN ENERGY.

Acknowledgments

Southern Review, "Seamstress"
Staple, "Hardwood Fire," "Looking at Turner's Oil on Canvas of the Doge Marrying the Sea"
The London Magazine, "Night Walk"
Stand, "Country Dance"
Poetry Review, "Something/Nothing," "Green Bananas Agenda - Staying Elsewhere"
Iota, "Bead Curtains"
New Delta Review, "I Collide With Saint Theresa and the Angel"
Pennine Ink, "Work"
New York Times and *New York Times Book of Verse*, "Query"
Times Literary Supplement, "Caught," "Windmills-Sails"
Geoffrey Dearmer Award, "Green Bananas"

Contents

ANYTHING AND ITS SHADOW

If Only

Knowing now
how short life is
I can't get
over that we're alive—
now, this second
which is already gone.
If only I could pick
a bunch of wild
seconds in the field
and hand them
to you in a jelly jar
to admire over supper,
I'd do that, you
know I would, but
all I can give you
is this poem.

Eilean Mor

As always
it was the approach

that evening—
low sun swiping

the water bucketing
our Zodiac toward
the rose-washed
leviathan half sub-

merged in its late day
bath affixing our
quick amazement,
long steps cut there,

and we glided inside a
cave's secrets: guano
white washing rock,
gannets nesting, but

as always
it was the approach
that evening—
long light sweeping

along the muscular
dark beneath
us to the luminous
shock ahead.

Calendar

I have nothing
to do tomorrow;
wealth of time
I am moving

toward at the
speed of light;
treasure in
the now; blind

flash in its
moment; its
own fantasy
piece I live for,

that may not be
what I diced
for, but that'll
be my life.

Seamstress

I woke last night from dreamless sleep to hear
what in the distance sounded like barely audible
tuneless humming womanly and maternal.
Was it humming? Enough it sounded so, it was as
comforting. All was still. The time near
three o'clock when you can hear the landscape.
It's the landscape humming to me, I thought,
but the murmur could just have been a distant car,
a single driver on the long way home.
Was it intended, a radio turned way down,
or was it wind whispering unwilled and ending
casually as begun? Still, this low humming
took the night so like thread that my sleep, ripped
by sudden half-felt fright, was with that uncut
sound thought through, and I slept again
seamed all together in that long thought's dark.

Perhaps

Jitters over the land jitters over
the water jitters up in the sky
writing in smoke over the water
over the land and breaking up
on the mountain peaks then
gathering again in ravines of
snakes slithering & only wanting
to live but able to swallow
timid mammals whole who
also wanted to nibble just as long
as they could jitters of us
under the cool knife of a surgeon
who loves the drama of it
this is oxygen breath says a voice
& you wake up choices of being
a rabbit or rock—perhaps a
blade of grass that returns—yes

Hardwood Fire

Outside,
the gray wind's
dry monotony
keeps the bare trees
in dreary chorus.
Phantom hymns
persist over
abandoned pews.

I build a fire
and in the slowly
darkening room
there is nothing

else that matters
but the rage
of those hard-
wood flames.

Tête–à–tête

Waving to myself
in the glass door—
"Have a glass of
wine," I say, but I
answer, "Thanks,
but I already have
one." "Yours is
darker, probably a
better Merlot," I say.
"That's the way it
goes" glass me says,
pouring another as
evening drops in.

. . . and gone

A little darkness poem
going into the night
goes like this the little
darkness poem sitting
at the table a dark
pane reflecting it just
as though it were another
room in the house a
creaking house creaking
darkness, creaking
quiet. A little darkness
poem scared by dark
windows that reflect a
ghost room with a sheet
of paper on which fear
is written down in a
little darkness poem for
the night that is now.

Broth

What is the metaphor
for the soul
if not a broth rinsed

with onion,
garlic, mushroom,
celery, and

habanero—all the
different
sides of you lost to

a melding
barely simmering,
beatific joy.

You

That body
encasing
what I love.

Herbes de Provence

Each a queen in its jar
these grasses far now
from their plots—lavender,
thyme, tarragon, rosemary,
marjoram and sweet fennel
each pronouncing its own
originality before entering
the fray of their gabbling
scents that fills my kitchen
like a party of geniuses
leaving their dry state
waiting to get smashed.

Glass

Evening—the grass barely green—
my reflection on the glass door
in palimpsest above it. Are you

the spirit of the grass? We take on a
different life in the dimmer
light that catches us in the equivocal

glass—the walls are green
and the grass is now dimmer green
while I, in the glass, am outlined

in darker coal while the grass
will never know how much
I love you here alone on the sofa.

Dark now, and I am just a shade
on the glass, not reflecting
but only a shadow of what I was
when we were walking grass.

jmt - im

Rebuke

What's the matter with
you
that where you lie
now
you can't break out of
the earth?
Do you lack the force
of a crocus
that you can't bloom
again?

jmt - i.m.

Word

Barney trots up to me
& puts his paw on
my forearm—I know
what he wants—he
wants to go out, but he's
just been out & I tell
him I'm writing a poem—
go lie down—& he lies
down for a minute &
a half while I diddle
& dawdle on some words
then Barney comes
back his dark eyes looking
& shifting, looking &
shifting away from me
& I realize now how much
he wants to run out into
the ineffable night to for-
get he's a dog, while I
want to write a poem to
forget I'm a speck in this
uni-verse—word
meaning only one turn.

Emblem

And I could go on letting
the crows into my head along
with the flowers, but the gray
sky would weigh everything down
flattening colors and sounds

into a pressed bloom and a black
flight crushed in the pages of
a heavy bible telling the same
story with more and more words
ignoring what it has caught.

I Collide with Saint Theresa and the Angel

Nothing eternal
in these late autumn
mountains but
the moment of absolute
beauty. Sun fire
in the trees arouses
and plays me
like a viola. Clarity
in dark tones rounded
off. Maternal. Only
a squirrel moves.
Then a crow.
I am still, ravished
by the landscape. Saint Theresa
and the angel were in no
greater ecstasy. I am no saint
receiving this perfection
which is not for the faint
of heart. For my sins
I stay awake
and look and take it in.

Work

November with its gray silence
keeps me honest. The poverty leaves me
on my own. There are no sounds
in the valley that I can score and play
back from my mind's white space.
If there are notes, they are only a few crows
marking the distance. Leaves are gone:
dropped and raked. We are waiting
for snow, though it's flinty smell
is not in the air. It's eerily warm. Usually
by now cold hits our bones,
and we know the dead. Trees too
with their fishbone skeletons are buried
in the air. Only the larch: golden,
waving majestically continues its dance.
November is the time of silence,
broody space, patience with its small
jobs, when we do all the work of the year.

Green Bananas

Green bananas splayed out in a basket—
not a very elegant basket,
though it has a, more or less, graceful
handle (repaired with duct tape)
arced over a curved base. Still, it could be
a painting, duct tape and all, to show
how life really is, to show that green
bananas will lie down anywhere,
splayed out from a stem, broken
off from a huge bunch, chopped out
of a republic built on green
bananas. As I write, the fruit yellows
in the sour February light, and is entirely
the most beautiful thing I've seen
all day: green, with yellow wipes, black
nosed as a stuffed bear. Somewhere
there is sun enough to spring
these bananas to life, though they
were hacked down in their very prime
for me in my sunless, northern
kitchen. What other communion do
I need than with these gold-
turning green bananas, and with all
the hands and feet that laid them
in this basket. Here is our photograph.

. . . it was

the way a tree trunk bends
one way, then another way

then forks, then suddenly
turns in yet another direction,

just slightly, then splits, then
bursts into flutters of leaves

asking everybody in the wind
where are we—where, where?

Hot Dog

Where are you going to my pretty Made
in America, milking? Aw, come
on, don't look at me like that, milking
the poor of Asia with hopes and soaps.
But, everything's made in China, Officer,
for the poor of America. Battle of Dreams,
the streams red with dye. You're
thinking again. You swore not to do that.
It's bad for your skin. None off
my nose. Hey, I'll have a lil' a dat wid
ketchup! Catch up? Yeh, well you
just try! My dreams beat yours to lollipops.

Staying Elsewhere

Ecstasy is something I must keep
for myself, here on the rat surface
of November. Dark mountain peaks
cut into an expiring sky, broody
gray everywhere, stillness, the air
so cold it's close to flint, close
to the smell of a musket just shot
in a local replay of the local battle
of the Revolution. There is nothing
to support me in this emptiness,
this drop to black and white life
I could call despair save that I am
left alone to the sheer transport
of my own elation which I've kept
secret in a tree like any squirrel,
but, I take this moment to fly
elsewhere from the bare branch.

Country Dance

Taking his time walking in front of us
across the dirt road, a woodcock shuffles in place
with each step, ignoring our enormous car.
Shuffling stiffly, he hears only a New Orleans
stomp as he jerks out a long, scrawny, libidinous
neck making the music he walks by, feeling for
worms it seems, under the earth he walks on. I want
him to dance at my wake to celebrate the music
from glittery leaves, silence over a meadow, crunch
of tires on gravel, thud of a maple trunk falling,
jump of a squirrel close by some dead raccoon whose
face has the same gone look my mother had
the moment after her last breath. I want a woodcock
to strut the earth when I go for the worms
under the grass, the red leaves, the hard road.

Spines

My old books
are falling apart,
bursting their stitches,
the glue dried

out in crumbles—
my old friends,
how I've loved you;
though there used

to be somebody in
town who bound
books, there isn't
anymore; it's as

though there weren't
anymore doctors
and we fell apart in
each others hands.

Wait Staff

In the novel I am reading two
protagonists are caught
in a storm that knocks them

over—so I get up for a glass
of wine; this couple
can wait; they will wait;

they are in print, after all,
Oh, how we all long
to be in print, but

these characters don't; they
have no choice.
Ah, the patience of fictional

dependents who'll
wait, stuck in a tornado, for
as long as it takes.

Gift Wrap

Instead why not
read the dictionary,
opening it at random
to 'panic,' then

tracing on to 'panicle'
and into the 'pantalets'
going from the jitters
to a flower with irregular

branches, then a cut
to underdrawers with
ruffles—what could
be more entertaining

than all these exquisite
surprises in chic
black and white wrap?

Here

The way you once picked up
a stone and said, "Here," handing it
to me, another time—you mentioned
something, not anything grand or tragic—not
Akhmatova's ". . . a woman with lips blue
with cold . . . whispered . . . can you write this?"
Not that, no, but ". . . last night I was
hungry so I had a slice of toast, then,
I had another one . . ." a moment you
handed to me, and that I took.

Moving Rock

Yesterday I
placed a small
volcanic rock
in my card-size
sand garden,
and drew lines
away from it in
sunbeams, then I
connected those
lines in cobwebs
and stopped.
Today I took out
the rock, then
I rested.

Looking at Turner's oil on canvas of the Doge marrying the sea

To marry the sea—
I've often thought of it,
standing on the shore,
feet laved by the long arms
of the tide. It would
certainly be for love: the sweet
wish to tame that immense
great cradle of comforting terror.
Sacrifice. Pitiful trifles
from my candy box of treasures:
coins, a picture of my mother
exchanged in pledge at the ceremony.
The sea leaves a bone
from a submarine, a whale,
a bottle of water. It relinquishes
more damage than I do,
after all it's richer.

Chants

Beaks mend the air
with loopy stitches,
loose seams in silks
of petals and pollen

raising saffron robes
around the shrubs and
against the windows
in impious chants—

such frippery bumps
the cold's severity—
now the land scatters
its heft and flings

away all its tedious
winter opinions. Why
teach our goofy trees
responsibility when

they want to fritter
and toss out time in
utter mess and nobody
pick it up, ditch it in

the air with no pause
on the old scabbed
leaves, dour rocks
that lose their songs?

Bead Curtains

There is, in the patience of this rain, an infinite
wisdom coming down as it does after
a long silence, a long withholding of itself
so far up in the sky it was beyond reckoning,
and everything in its dryness was deadly
beautiful, so much died in its absence:
creatures unheard of lived and died
under rocks, beneath trees, throughout
bushes, in tilled fields prepared for the next
crop that browned, twisted, sank and
rotted down in the parched soil too exhausted
to notice, too delirious to cradle the shoots
after the dark womb's gestation. There is,
in the patience of this rain, an infinite wisdom,
falling straight down in strings, like the entrance
to a fortune teller's room behind the candle
shop on Main Street, knowing how much is in store
for the future, how much of the past it brings.

Composition

Sounds attacked me:
droning car engines in the valley,
a chainsaw next door,
downstairs a painter's whistle;
I hated each one when
suddenly the whistling, some wind
chimes on the porch and
the slow beat of the valley worrying
together were scorned
by the scour of the chainsaw
and I took down the score.

After a Long Winter

The way dead leaves
danced across

the lawn was the
Ballet Russe for me.

Spring

Each pane of glass
in the window
an abstraction
I'll cut out and sell
for a good price.

Dracula in the Morning

Sudden oddity
of black stick
legs struggling
round a half-shut

casement window;
such limbs alive
pipe cleaners long
as a dragonfly's on

a crinkly bat's body,
or magician's black
cloth dropped to hide
tricks—this terrorist

so small now so
offenseless flailing
useless wings
in futile efforts at

shape-shifting to
spring free from
a window's grasp
in escape as smoke.

Paper Joy

An odd one
fluttered among
the gulls above
Lexington Avenue

bunched—it
suddenly unfurled
to a ribbon—
spiraled—spread

wings aloft
over the terrible
asphalt—in loops
it took the gusts

between buildings—
you grumbling
the traffic—me
up in the very air.

Castle

Exquisitely carved
by beaks
a maple stump

was turned
into a castle from
a fairy tale

the illustration
showing
it's lift from

ground so green
and dark as
to betray its force

as it rose in
blades and grottos
of peaked

pyramidal rise—
each incise
cutting the air.

Grande Dame

Wild elegance,
try to beat it—that grande
dame turkey hen
extending one spidery foot
after another, long
thin legs—beige down
her back, iridescent bronze
of the wing feathers
and bosom prow,
pointy high-button shoes
from Italy. Slowly
she circles the feeder, then,
reassured, eats
the seeds we've spread
for her. Soon she'll disappear
in a cloud of gnats
off into the underbrush.

. . . but music is time you can play again

I have control
over my actions

but none over
now—which is

already gone—
as I decide to

pick up a fork,
my hand ages

without asking
for permission—

no reason to be
nervous—it'll

happen anyway.
There you go—

Query

What would it be
like to enter
a day which was
an immense cube
of colorless, un-
flavored gelatin?

Perish the Thought

As my head
drops

from the chop
block,

I think of
going

to America.

Peanut Butter Poem

You know how it is when your spoon
scrapes the bottom of the peanut butter
jar & there just isn't enough to tide
you over until the next thought & all
there is in you is a feeling of emptiness
which may be lack of ineffable arms
entwining you in the cold you shiver in
though it's 80 degrees in the shade
of an old maple tree you grew up under
that was your mother & your father
it's shivering leaves your entertainment
until autumn when your tree lost
itself such that you also lost envelope
to send out to a world whose stamp was
the face of an uncompromising figure
when all you wanted was a little
compromise between yourself & dark.

Dinner

Cold oatmeal &
a glass of Chablis;

such a Schumann
fantasiestücke

menu; an absolute
balance between

mad & sane here;
now is the weird

stay & the furnace
sounding the walls.

Barcarole

Mandolins
strummed by

pangolins in
a gondola

olin ola ola
in silken

night air.

Something/Nothing

Finally, on a park bench: dappled sun
through summer leaves, little birds
darting through them as though
threading a fragile material made of
gold light and dark lace in a complicated
weaving of thoughts my fingers are not
deft enough to handle, but that I can reflect
on in a complicated process descending
from the folds of my brain. I am glad to be
good for something as evening approaches.
The light and the dark play on me. I am
pure instrument: all reed, strings, winds,
drum. Everything has its way with me.
Nothing has happened. I have waited
so long for nothing to happen.

Cognac

Sip it as the sun
goes down on
a Paris sidewalk
café as all you
want is to
get away from
yourself &
do nothing but
watch Gérard
de Nerval walking
his lobster
in a quiet drama
that's free.

Nuts and Bolts

Cracked &
drove off a
2 inch cliff.

plots

grass is such a slut
slinking around roses,

over ashes, getting
its hair done once a

week to keep an edge
over living and dead

Caught

A couple that drinks
together, stays
together we say making
sure the level of
each glass is equal

as we dream through
a bottle of Chablis
which doesn't quite have
that ultimate dry pop
but still triggers little

angels in the interstices
of our brains, the folds
lighting up red and
peach colored below
the awful authority

we have sacked
for the night as we
celebrate nothing in
particular other than
that the night is dark

and huge and also
awful, such that all
mediation runs awry
and we are caught
back in the candlelight.

Night Walk

Weaving giddily and quite drunkenly across
the dirt road walking home from the party
we held on to each other

giggling and stepping on each other's
toes and kicking small stones out into the bushes
that lined the road;

tall trees darkened in the full moonlight holding
themselves up for us as models
of virtue which we delightedly

knew we were not. We held a flashlight
that caught pairs of
low eyes off deep in the bushes and while we laughed

we caught these in our
eyes, received these unthinkingly in our
minds—they were only pairs of small reflections

after all,
pairs of the way light goes into a camera
onto an innocent plate.

On the Bus

As she talks
to the man
across the aisle,
she twists,
untwists a paper-
clip, first
one hand on top,
then the other;
fingertips kiss
in the enterprise.

After the Rain

Nestled in the stamens
of a tiger lily
ladybugs getting it on.

Drops of water
on the petals blessing
their cunning.

Windmills – Sails

In Cap Chat, Gaspé, Canada
there are a hundred windmills covering
every whim of the winds—placed,
as they are, on the rolling hills there
bordering the Saint Lawrence River.
The windmills surround Aeolius,
called the father of all windmills, being
the tallest in the world, but it should
be called the mother for its womb-
shaped, curved-steel arcs that catch
the currents like lyres. No breeze goes
uncaught; no cough vanishes unused;
air's every shiver grasped fully—
that happens too with the sails of the
four-masted schooner docked nearby,
a sail poised for every whistle; I noticed
this on the model ship in the restaurant
where we ate mussels piled high
in their bowls in that town set in one
of those little arced bays, formed by
the wind and the water, protecting
a tin-steepled church that leads
the low houses like a mother hen.
Everything is caught, everything is led;
everything is fashioned into a thing
that is useful in this harsh, steep land
where nobody lives in the hills
alone. Boats go out just so far, then
turn back before dark to town.

Celebration

Everybody in Paris is
serving in a bowl.
we read, and it came; a
head cum; together—
first in colors: black, pink
green, then shapes:
arcs, ovals, cylinders;
but it's got to taste good,
you said. O that I said.
It needs sauce, you said.
You loved sauce, yes,
though it did need
something under it. You
were the sauce, my
darling, and I—well, I
was the avocado so
together we wrote a recipe
for a bowl: black rice,
salmon, avocado topped
by La Marseillaise.

im - jmt

Zucchero, sugar, sucre, azucar, zucker

We are all here in this hamlet
waiting for the painting,
stirring sugar in five languages
into espresso. We are all
here in a hamlet near Arezzo
waiting for the door
to open to Piero's Madonna
del Parte so we can see
the woman in blue delicately
fingering the buttons of the dress
that encloses the child.
Her eyes know only interiors.
Guards switch on the lights.
Angels pull back the curtains.
We gasp in five languages.
The painting mends
the isolations of our tongues.

Anything & Its Shadow

Took a picture of a crumpled
napkin this evening—
maybe an iceberg, maybe Mont Blanc—

amazing what you can find
before you toss it.

Just think of what the garbage
collector has on his
truck as he drives away—anything

& its shadow is wondrous.
Ignore the odor of a dead fish—

look at its skeleton—
so simple, so elegant, so spare
compared to ours.

Mirror Selfie

You are
all there is

of you
in the entire

universe
I said

to the quiet
face.

Ode

three cheers
for our tiny
lives in this
vast universe

Done

Done quietly as a still pond
impinged by a stone,

circles spreading out
to you, my love,

tangles of lost roots there
at the only shore.

for Jim

I know what I have given you . . .
I do not know what you have received.

—ANTONIO PORCHIA